Simple as a Sonnet

Simple as a Sonnet

Poems by

Lisa DeSiro

Cover design by Shay Culligan

ISBN: 978-1-952326-94-3

Kelsay Books
502 South 1040 East, A-119
American Fork, Utah, 84003

*To the exes
and the single ladies*

Acknowledgments

I'm grateful to the editors of the following publications in which these poems first appeared, some as earlier versions or with different titles.

The Avenue: "Learning to Rumba," "Naked & Clothed"
Commonthought Magazine: "Alter Ego," "Hooking Up Aubade,"
    "Retraction," "Static Cling"
The Hampden-Sydney Poetry Review: "Be My Valentine"
Mezzo Cammin: "Imagined Advice from Edna St. Vincent Millay"
Right Hand Pointing (One Sentence Poems): "Minus +1"
Prodigal's Chair: "Forbidden Fruit," "Hindsight," "Notation,"
    "Self-Repairing," "Shedding," "The Other Woman Confesses,"
    "The Survivor Exorcises an Evil Spirit"
Shooter Literary Magazine: "Dating through the Decades," "The
    Party Girl Warns Her Heart"

"The Survivor Exorcises an Evil Spirit" was also printed in *Nasty Women Poets: An Unapologetic Anthology of Subversive Verse* (Lost Horse Press, 2017).

Musical settings of "Living Alone" and "Naked & Clothed" are included on the album *Living in Light* (Albany Records, 2017).

The last line of "Forbidden Fruit" refers to Louise de Vilmorin's poem "Violon."

Special thanks:

Karen Kelsay, Delisa Hargrove, and everyone at Kelsay Books/White Violet Press for bringing this book into the world.

Allison Adair, Jenna Le, and Deborah Schwartz for reading the manuscript and providing such generous statements of support.

Kali Pezzi, who read an early version of this collection and offered kind encouragement.

Kathleen McClung, who awarded Second Prize to "Imagined Advice from Edna St. Vincent Millay" in the 2013 Soul-Making Keats Literary Competition, sonnet category.

Heather Gilligan, Joel Kenneth Boyd, and David DeSiro (my brother) for so creatively setting some of these poems to music.

The steadfast (girl)friends who have thus far outlasted all my boyfriends: Sue, Gwen, Robin, Brian, Anastasia, Lorna, Sara, Kay, Ann, Brenna, Vartan, Michael, Brad, Kerry, Esther, Janine, Samia, Cat, Tzarina.

Contents

The ABCs of How to Catch a Man

Always look your best.
Behave like a lady.
Cook him a hearty meal.
Diet if necessary.
Enthusiasm is an asset.
Flirt, but don't overdo it.
Give your full attention when he's talking.
Have a sense of humor. But don't be too smart:
Intellect might intimidate him.
Just be yourself.
Keep your options open.
Let him open doors and pay for dinner. Stay cheerful:
Moodiness is a turn-off.
No nagging, either. Allow him to
Order for you at restaurants.
Put on make-up and perfume.
Quiet girls: don't be shy.
Rambunctious girls: don't be bossy.
Smile often and laugh at his jokes.
Thank him after every date.
Understand that he works hard.
Vary your topics of conversation. Don't be dull.
Wear sexy clothes and high heels.
XO only if he does so first.
Yield gracefully, when the time is right. And remember:
Zingy women will get the most attention.

Static Cling

down in the basement
               laundry room
somebody transferred
               my hot clothes
from washer to dryer
               maybe Pylon (red hair)
or Skin (uncircumcised)
               or one of the other nick-
names wheeling kegs
               through co-ed hallways
getting girls like me
               drunk on Bo-Jos
(beer & orange juice)
               but one helped pick up
the pieces when my mug
               smashed it was
Crazy John who now
               appears shirtless & tan
reaching a hand lifting
               a single sock stuck
to panties *Oh sorry*
               are these yours?

Coupled

When we finally "slept" together, we heard
weird noises, during and afterward:
yodeling-yowling cats right
outside the window. *Is it a fight?*
I asked. *Mating,* he said, with a grin.
Like us. Except we're committing a sin.
Our laughter filled the chilly hollow
room; abrupt silence followed.
Against my cheek I felt his heart
ticking like a clock. He started
twitching in his sleep, the way
an animal does when it dreams. I lay
still, clutching him, wide awake.
Had we made love, or made a mistake?

Passenger & Driver

Because I want this man
to be holding my hand
rather than the gear-
shift, I reach out, thread
my fingers through his hair.
When he shakes his head,
dog-like, and frowns—quick,
I withdraw. Flicks
of rain begin.
I watch the wind-
shield wipers sweep.
Swallow words. He keeps
his eyes on the road.
Several more miles to go.

Notation

Money's tight. I only spend time
alone in my cheap sublet studio,
listening to a mixed tape he made,
turning it over and over, replaying…
Before our first real gig, we split

a pitcher. Happy hour. Gathering gear
(keyboard, guitar, amps, cables wedged
behind heavy collapsible risers) slack-
limbed, laughing, we couldn't dislodge
a thing. *How can we get this shit out?*

I shouted, climbing the pile of equipment.
Slipped and fell. Could have broken my
neck if he hadn't caught me. *Partial to
what?* might have been his remark if he
could have seen the partial lunar eclipse

this evening, here, with me. He's missing
a second phenomenon now: the slats
of the window-blind form a grand staff
where the full moon floats like a perfect
whole note drawn between parallel lines.

Hindsight

Looking back, does no good for me
to ask *How could you not see…?*
The irony: his name was Tom.
He was a starving-artist drummer
who talked dirty and confessed
his daily struggle with depression,
then revealed another foible:
late-night looking into people's
windows. Which was worse, his crime
of peeping or to sleep with him?
Eyes closed, I stroked his bumpy frail
spine like I was reading braille.
We both were blind. And guilty of
wanting love; wanting; love.

Learning to Rumba

I saw a flyer posted,
took the free trial.
Believed the cute teacher,
all compliments and smiles:

You seem like a natural.
I bought the package deal:
weekly private lessons.
I wore 3-inch heels,

tight flared pants,
mini skirts that swirled,
shirts that showed my midriff.
Same as the other girls.

The teacher—muscular,
short, blond, Danish,
drenched with cologne—
spoke accented English,

shouted at us. *Chest up!*
Move your hips! Come on!
Scrutinized our bodies
in the mirrors as we spun.

Non-stop from the stereo,
loud music pumped:
bass, drums, piano,
accordion, trumpet.

My favorite was rumba:
quick—quick—slow,
right—left—right…
I felt which way to go

by the guidance of his palm
pressed against my back,
his fingers clasping mine.
I picked the steps up quick.

He said: *You follow well,*
better than the other students.
You keep your grip firm.
You understand resistance.

In the dim practice room
at the end of the hall—
door closed, just us—
he leaned against the wall,

smoked a cigarette,
flicked it to the floor.
You're the perfect height…
We did nothing more

than make out, grope each other,
fully clothed, fast and rough.
So I thought that was that.
But I hadn't learned enough.

Naked & Clothed

Caressing his neck,
shoulders, back, chest, abdomen...
I want to sprout leaves,
send tendrils all over him
like a vine covers a wall.

Locked in the bathroom
of the bus, upright, pants down:
posthaste and jolted.

The One Who Got Away

That day I passed by the café he was working
and ran out to the sidewalk shouting my name
and I turned not knowing who had called, but then
so happy to see him so happy to see me.

He ran out to the sidewalk, shouting. My name
meant nothing without his. He proposed,
so happy. To see him so happy to see me
say yes was almost more joy than I could take.

I meant it, nothing without him. He proposed
post-coitus. We were young, in love. What else was there
to say? *Yes. More.* Joyful, I thought I could take
anything. Constant traveling. Absences. Everything,

post-coitus, forgiven. In young love, what else is there
except acceptance? Rowdy friends. Drinking. Drugs.
Anywhere he traveled, his absence filled everything
in our apartment. His drums and guitars. Waiting. Mute.

Except... I accepted friends, rowdy drinking, drugs,
a secret vial of Prozac stashed inside the top drawer.
In our apartment, all his instruments mutely waited
while I played my piano — a gift from him.

Prozac for the vile inside. Top-secret stash. A drawer,
a woodworker, he sketched and then built a bench
for my piano — one of many gifts from him. We played,
we practiced, we listened to so much music…

A worker. A sketch. The wooden bench he built
became symbolic after he moved out. Like every
piece of music I listened to or practiced… So much
hurt. I lost myself with him. He was lost. Who he used to be

became a symbol. I moved out, after. Every
corner I turned not knowing if he would call. But by then
he was hurt, lost within his mind. Lost, who used to be
that boy working in the café where I passed by.

Forbidden Fruit

I held the hem of my skirt above my knees,
exposing my bare legs to the breeze
and sidelong looks of the man with whom
I strolled among exotic blooms.
He admired their fragrances, their lush
colors, though he was suffering, flushed
and sweaty under the sun's blaze
because he wore all black. His gaze
met mine, lingered. I gave, unasked,
the only thing I could: a flask
of water. He took it, trembling, and drank.
And when he offered me his thanks
I thought of that poem in French, comparing
the love-struck heart to a strawberry.

Shedding

A dog's brain has no capacity
for inhibition because its frontal lobe
is too small, he told me. *See—*

He gestured toward the yellow Lab
who kept pawing my lap, not afraid
to show desire, pleading for any scrap.

Just like before, he'd made
dinner: spaghetti, salad, fresh bread.
The usual. Then he played

his latest songs. We drank a red,
dry, Italian vintage. He refilled
my glass readily but couldn't read

the signals: how I was willing,
if not exactly able, to guzzle the sound
of his amplified voice. Spilling

my real thoughts, as I spun around
in his leather swivel chair, rather
than saying I loved the music—no, my mind

couldn't make my mouth speak. Bothered,
hot in my knit-wool burgundy dress,
I endured the parlor trick: a round cracker,

like a large communion wafer, placed
on the dog's tongue after he commanded *Sit.*
He intoned *Body of Christ* and yes,

I laughed as the silly creature ate it
and then lay between us while we watched
Woody Allen movies. *Look at your feet,*

he said. *You can tell how much
she sheds.* My stockings had grown beards,
sprouted whitish-yellow tufts.

He apologized because they appeared
to be stuck, like tiny thorns, throughout
my dress, too. I felt his breath on my ears

as he stood behind me holding my coat.
This dress fits you well, he said. *Stay.
Lie down. Behave.* That's what

he told the dog. I wanted him to say
those things to me, not drive me home.
Not loan me a new translation of Dante.

Not take another walk along the same
path after Mass, going nowhere
every Sunday, discussing another poem.

I had to wash my clothes a lot before
they finally shed that damn dog's hair.

Hooking Up Aubade

Early riser, no alarm required,
he lurches out of bed, girds himself
with yesterday's briefs, slings his guitar
across his bare torso. His singing
is like his body: rustic but in tune.

Despite my need to pee I stay
and listen, naked under the sheets.
Mere hours ago it was all
mumbled words, fumbling hands,
eyes half-closed. Half-hearted,

his caresses. He wouldn't undress
either of us. I did. Everything.
After, he fell asleep. He snored.
So cliché—dawn, open window,
bird chirps, summer breeze,

his drunken wheezing. Now
he stacks music on my stomach,
pages of chord progressions and lyrics.
We smile as they pile up. But I'm
remembering my dream:

the first man tried to attack me,
the second man ran to rescue me,
and both were him. I turned from them,
peering through tears at a mirror,
a blurred reflection—not mine,

some younger woman's face
behind a bridal veil. She woke me
with a whisper. *You were never
his intended. You will never be
the prize he wants to win.*

The Party Girl Warns Her Heart

If when I've had one
too many you become
            bloated and start
                        flinging
            yourself pathetically against
my ribcage wanting to break
                        loose and if subsequent
                        drenching
            doesn't slake your thirst
nor stop your slobbering
                        you bloody
                        beaten thing
            just remember
once you're soaked
                        with high-proof stuff
                        all it takes is a single match
            for you
to get
                        burned
                        again

Alter Ego

She only drinks drinks whose names end in vowels:
margarita, mojito, martini.
She has perfect vision, eyes wise as an owl's.
She looks fabulous in a bikini.
She dresses in dresses whose cut always flatters
her figure: elegant, hip.
She knows it's today, not tomorrow, that matters.
She always leaves a big tip.
She's the girl who remains on Saturday nights
when "last call" is announced at a bar.
Her gentlemen minions get into fights
over who takes her home in whose car.
Let them fuss and fume and try to decide,
she thinks. *I'm taking them all for a ride.*

The Other Woman Confesses

i.

I'd get turned on even before the foreplay.
He was methodical. Meticulous.
Tugging loose my ponytail.
Deftly, with one hand, unhooking
either back- or front-close bras.
Peeling away my tightest jeans, chuckling.

Our motions unmoored the bed, pillows
pushed overboard. Or we made it
only as far as the living room,
contortionists on the love seat. Or
he pressed me against the doorjamb,
or laid me across the kitchen table.

We always held each other a little while,
stroking skin and continuing to kiss (I'm sorry
for telling you this) before he got up
to throw away the condom.
Toilet flushing. Tremors, my legs
twitching as I watched him get dressed.

ii.

Once, he let himself fall asleep.
Splayed on top of me,
his breathing laborious.
His stubbled cheek made my neck itch.
Beneath his warm weight, I shifted
and saw his face transformed:
eyes closed, frowning, older.
I wondered if he was thinking about you.

iii.

He was with me the night you went into labor.
I never felt jealous.
Envious, a little.
Nothing growing inside me except guilt.

I hoped it would be a girl. I said to myself
Maybe then he'll change his ways.
Believe me. As much as I wanted him,
I wanted him, for your sake, to change.

Or for my sake.
Or for his own.

Self-Repairing

In the dream I was wearing
my patent-leather red
shoes, and not caring
if they got wet as we waded

through waves by the shore.
The ocean seethed
through an open door.
We barely breathed.

The tide rolled out like fog.
He followed at my heels
like a well-trained dog.
Held, I could feel

his tell-tale swell. My grip
tightened. His zipper
got stuck.
Just my luck.

Imagined Advice from Edna St. Vincent Millay

Staying friends with lovers can be done.
All you need is patience and finesse.
Say you've got yourself in a bit of a mess
with two gentlemen admirers: one
who "isn't really single" and one
who decides that he "well, more or less"
would prefer remaining single. A stress-
provoking situation, although fun
might be had… But if things have gone
far enough with both men, the key to success-
fully being platonic (which might depress
the most resilient heart, when left alone)
is this: write until you stop dwelling on it.
You see? Simple. Simple as a sonnet.

Be My Valentine

We take a Sunday stroll. It's almost dusk.
Clouds clumsily obscure the rising half-
moon. Ice crystals fill the air, like dust.
Gusts of wind follow us along the path.
Other walkers nod and smile, say hello;
dogs, with wagging tails, sniff our hands.
But the children riding sleds down the snow-
covered hill, freed from weekday demands,
don't notice us. Focused on their fun,
they seem blissfully oblivious of time.
Undisturbed by the soon-setting sun,
they slide to the bottom and they climb
up again, then make the same trip all over.
So does the sun. And the moon. So do lovers.

Seasonal Monogamy

Most of the ducks
who flocked to this dock

this winter afternoon
are sleeping in the sun,

but these two doze
in the shadows.

He has a green sheen.
She's dull brown.

Bent-backward necks,
bills tucked

under feathers.
They stand together,

both balancing one-
legged on

a single splayed foot,
rooted.

Two of a kind, like we
used to be.

Metamorphosis

It's Kafka-esque, this awful sense of dread
as I brush and floss and wash. Hard to say
which role you'll pick tonight for me to play
before I get undressed and get in bed.
The cruel tormented lover? Tender groom?
When at last you let me fall asleep, I dream
I'm babysitting children. One, a boy,
is crawling unattended. *Look out!* I cry,
afraid he'll harm himself. But then a little
girl tackles him gently, with a hug,
onto the wide plush oriental rug.
He lies there on his back like a beetle,
flailing arms and legs. Not hard to see
which one symbolizes you, which me.

Demons & Decapitation

The stairs were wide, uneven, stone or clay, carved with gargoyles.
Their faces were magnificent, intricate, expressive.
We ascended by stepping on their shoulders.
I kept looking down until you took me by the hand.
These are my angels, you explained.
They scare away demons from my mind.

Later, I sat on a bench and you forced a helmet over my head.
I yielded because you were wielding a hand saw.
First, with the flat side, you whacked my neck until it was numb.
Then, with the blade, you started scratching beneath my chin.
Your words were muffled: *Don't be afraid.*
This way we both get what we want.

When I try to tell this dream at breakfast you yell at me.

Retraction

I take it back, what I said.
I have no problem with my bed.
The full-size width is adequate
room for me, and for my cat.
The firm mattress doesn't make
my hip or neck or shoulders ache.
No, I don't need a topper
made of memory foam or rubber.
No, I don't need a queen.
And no, the pillows aren't too lean.
And no, the covers aren't too thin.
And no use arguing again
'cause there's no problem with my bed.
Don't think, even for one minute,
there's a problem with my bed.
I sleep just fine without you in it.

The Survivor Exorcises an Evil Spirit

Although he and I were through,
there was no mistaking who
the hulking creature represented
in my nightmare. First it bent
over me—monstrous, awful—
then it shrank, became a skull.
So I shoved it to the floor
and chased it through the bedroom door.
Screaming *Go away! Get out!*
and brandishing a baseball bat,
I bashed and bashed and bashed that head
until the ugly thing was dead.
I woke up scared. But not in pain.
I never dreamt of him again.

Trick or Treat

We met at a bar Halloween night,
masked by drunkenness, costumed:
fake Oktoberfest lederhosen,
sexy Little Red Riding Hood.
Not what I'd call auspicious. But
of course it felt romantic

saying *Let's get out of here,*
kissing on a park bench in the rain,
staggering toward the subway
with arms around each others' waists.
Other details I didn't remember
the next day, such as: the ring

found on the street. He texted
photos for proof and when next
we met up, he presented me with this
fake-gold spike-studded full-finger band.
Not my style or my size. But
of course I tried it on.

The Middle-Aged Taurus Laments

"Hey baby, what's your sign?"
used to be the pick-up line.
Things were easier back then.
You could ask potential men
their date of birth, then try them out.
I tried: a Capricorn (lusty goat);
a water-bearer Aquarius
(slippery fish); a Sagittarius
(restless archer); even, once,
a Leo (sweetly roaring dunce)—
and more. All incompatible.
And now who'd want to pet the bull
I've become?
                    Screw the stars.
My planet's Venus. Men *are* from Mars.

Minus +1

At this
garden party,

among partners
& husbands
& wives
& boyfriends
& girlfriends,

and a
couple of
bees pollinating
butterfly bushes,

and a
pear tree
bearing fruit
in pairs,

I take
comfort from

a
lone
marigold
showing
her
brave
face
among
the
weeds.

Living Alone

one is affected most
not by the singleness,
the lack of company,
but by the absence
of conversation
which leaves room only

for thought.
The danger is that
what the mind creates
the body accepts as real—
such is the power of imagination.
Even when the body escapes in sleep,

the mind doesn't know how to stop
and continues its busywork
in the form of dreams. Thus
day and night,
waking and sleeping,
one is tormented.

The intellect understands
sometimes
it is better
to let go;
the heart always wants
to hold on.

In-between,
one's life takes shape.

Match

The ampersands of chance
link us all by happenstance.
Everyone's in on the joke:
straight as laces, queer as folk;
Tinder, J Date, OK Cupid;
wicked smart & dumb-ass stupid;
Shit Together & Hot Mess.
Random as a game of chess—
forward, sideways, up & down,
maneuvering to gain the crown—
we plot to capture queens & kings.
But we're pathetic pawns. Poor things,
we play for keeps, hoping fate
might turn a date into check-mate.

Dating through the Decades

i. 20-something

I brought home a guy from a bar.
He was only in town for the weekend.
He'd been flirting with my friend.
(The dress I was wearing belonged to her.)
When she rebuffed, he turned to me.
We went outside behind a tree
and did a bit of this and that…
and then the other, back at my flat.

ii. 30-something

I brought home a guy from a party.
He was the hostess's husband's friend.
(The vodka shots had made me weaken.)
He mistook me for under thirty.
When I walked past, he grabbed my wrist.
We went outside and smoked and kissed
and found some other things to do
indoors. He had a large…tattoo.

iii. 40-something

I brought home a guy after dinner.
He was a "profile fit" online
and by our second glass of wine
it seemed I'd found myself a winner.
Funny, smart, full head of hair,
plus knew his way around "down there."
He even stayed the night. And then
I never heard from him again.

iv. Conclusion

So much for sex on the first date.
Perhaps, indeed, better to wait.
But if I start being thrifty
now, what will happen by age fifty?

Sleeping Together

I love how our bodies fit
so snugly, front
pressed against back, knee
tucked behind knee, arm
draped over waist.

I love the sound as your
breathing changes
as you slip into
dreams, your fingers flutter-
touching mine.

I love the warm waking
when our eyes
open and find each other,
our smiles
becoming a kiss.

I love the bliss
of the two of us doing it
literally, like this.

I Love You in Three Languages

It's such a simple thing. To say
Te amo, Ich liebe dich, Je t'aime—
in any way. On any day
it's such a simple thing to say
these words. Yet how much they convey
when both of us are saying them.
It's such a simple thing to say:
Te amo. Ich liebe dich. Je t'aime.

New Year's Resolution

The frozen snow crushed by our feet
is loud: we speak, then must repeat
ourselves. You lead the way, winding
through shadowed trees. A step behind,
I follow your tracks over ground glazed
like sweet confection. Twilight haze
hushes the air when we stand still,
catching our breath. Bliss fills
my body, warming all my core
as we kiss—then kiss more
until we laugh—Silly us,
in the woods! Love is ridiculous.
And yet, how sublime
at last to be a pair who rhyme.

Almost

I thought we were a pair in rhyme.
Not just dating; true soulmates,
the planet Venus both of ours.
I dreamt this never would happen again.
Which blame belongs to you, which me?
Lovers do as the sun and the moon.
Sonnets are simpler. You see,
I think you've taken me for a ride.
Bitten my stricken heart like a berry,
wanting …? Love, I was wanting
to go several more miles.
Make no mistake: we had love.

About the Author

Lisa DeSiro is the author of two previous collections: *Labor* (Nixes Mate, 2018) and *Grief Dreams* (White Knuckle Press, 2017). Her poetry is featured in *Writers Resist: The Anthology, Nasty Women Poets: An Unapologetic Anthology of Subversive Verse,* and *Thirty Days: The Best of the Tupelo Press 30/30 Project's First Year;* as well as in various journals such as *The Hampden-Sydney Poetry Review, Lily Poetry Review, Mezzo Cammin, Mom Egg Review, The Ocean State Review, Ovunque Siamo, Rattle (Poets Respond), Salamander, Shooter Literary Magazine,* and others. Her poem "Motherly Advice" was nominated for a 2019 Pushcart Prize by *The Orchards Poetry Journal* and her poem "In Lieu of Flowers" was a winner in the 2017 City of Cambridge Sidewalk Poetry Contest. Her texts have also been set to music by several composers and recorded on two albums. Along with an MFA in Creative Writing from Lesley University, Lisa has degrees from Binghamton University, Boston Conservatory, and Longy School of Music. Her career has included working for academic and non-profit organizations as an accompanist, teacher, administrator, production assistant, and editor. She is founder/host of the Solidarity Salon, a performance series featuring multi-genre artists who are women, people of color, immigrants, LGBTQ+, and/or persons with disabilities. Read more about Lisa at thepoetpianist.com.

www.ingramcontent.com/pod-product-compliance
Lightning Source LLC
Chambersburg PA
CBHW071359090426
42738CB00012B/3171